MILDRED **HUNT**

MODERN DAY
Principles

SHAPE UP **AMERICA**

WORKBOOK PRESS LLC
187 E Warm Springs Rd,
Suite B285, Las Vegas, NV 89119, USA

Website: https://workbookpress.com/
Hotline: 1-888-818-4856
Email: admin@workbookpress.com

Ordering Information:
Quantity sales. Special discounts are available on quantity purchases by corporations, associations, and others. For details, contact the publisher at the address above.

ISBN-13:   978-1-958176-15-3 (Paperback Version)

REV. DATE: 04/05/2022

MODERN DAY PRINCIPLES:

Shape Up America

Mildred Hunt

DEDICATION PAGE

First, let me start by giving thanks to Jehovah my leader and Jesus my advisor. Without my relationship with my spiritual council, I wouldn't have been able to acknowledge rights from wrongs.

Secondly, I want to give a dedication to my 3 wonderful children, Tykese, Robbie, and Ocee. My love mate Jermaine and his auntie RIP Ella Williams. My sister Susie. My best friend Mr. J. Davis.

Lastly, my family and friends for the support and believing in my talent.

Chapter 1

<u>Right & Wrong</u>

Life is full of unexpected surprises. From birth to death, there are obstacles and trials we all must face, either together or as one individual person. Building bonds and breaking down bad bridges is the key to a healthy successful Christian life. With the Heavenly Father as your ruler and King Jesus as your personal savior, trusting and believing that time can't bring you nothing your soul can't handle.

As a child hopefully in church, you are built up to withstand storms and test from negativity. Your guardian teaches you to strengthen and self-worth to protect yourself from all others. Elementary school through middle school, you learn about respect for authorities, and the first door opens your mind about learning. Patterns of behavior, communication, and emotions all developed by age 12. Once you start leaving your parents' door and exploring the world on your own, at this age, all that you have learned is where everybody begins to judge you and lead you into your youth adulthood.

This Earth is a gain to your little life. You think, "you

know everything about life", once your self-consciousness is developed, "Nobody can tell you nothing"; "you start smelling you must", is what my elders classified it as. While when you're a child, nobody understands how you really view life and see other through your judgmental mind frame. You feel like a robot or puppet with all those hand in on raising you up. All those opinions, rules, guidelines, extra adult like leaders, involved then, most will disappear by the time you turn 19. Don't worry nor focus on them long. Believe half and listen to all while you can. I'm 36 now, and still processing most of what I was taught as a child and youth adult. If not for the bible and TV, I would be in a graveyard in hell, trying to be a perfect little person on Earth.

There is really a fine line in the sand between right and wrong. Then dealing with right and wrong, there's consequences to every action or decision your mind makes up. That's stressful enough to worry, depress, or fear anybody out of their own mind. When you are born with a purpose and start seeing your dreams in the future ahead of your time, it is hard following others' structured lifestyle, which may be different then what you perceive now about yourself in the next few years. These are what's causing difficulties in raising a child and living as a child in this world. In your head, you must find some commendable balance and grounds to fit in your life so you can understand the concern of all your leaders and peers. All these saying like "The skies are your limits", "You'll wish you'll never do that", or "Hard head makes a soft behind" are as old as my grandmother's church shoes. Every day marks a new beginning of life. What worked back then sure won't help you now, when the world is growing cooler by the breath of a new baby being born. Time changes, so does individual mind frame by the second. A real monster is being created on your left, while a real angle is in the making on your right, while you're playing in your own imaginations, when hanging with the neighbors' children from the right and left apartment. Influence of outsiders is what you call it. You have even more pressure now you got to fit in with the outside world. Here are some helpful thoughts that should help you overcome this stage of life:

- When you hear a negative word or piece of advice, accept it in your heart. Let it roll out your ear, like that conversation never took place in your life.
- When family disappoints you? Don't let them get under your skin. Remember that the only perfect person that ever walked the face of this Earth is and always will be King Jesus Christ. Negativity doesn't get any power in this world. Nor enough time in Hell to mess up your life story.

- When your haters/enemies speak badly about you, simply shake off their views and delete them out of your life. Don't hold on to bad bridges, burn them. Free yourself of dead weight in your mind.
- When doubt hits your mind, don't dwell on it. Talk to somebody. Pray for the Heavenly Father to come bail you out of those troubled times.
- Life does seem to get smaller the more you practice learning from past mistakes.
- Protect yourself. Keep your mind open and your feet above the ground, in other words be focused all the time, and pay attention.
- Save room in your heart and mind to grow up.
- You can only control yourself and those younger than you. Respect even when you feel uncertain about somebody.
- Respect your community and pitch in wherever you can to help somebody build their life up. If they don't want your advice, then pray they get it for themselves one day.
- Don't explain yourself to strangers. Especially if they're not a part of your everyday life nor will they be a part of your future.
- Spend time with those that bring positive energy into your life
- Never be too sure of yourself. We learn from each other as examples of life. With every breath in your body, keep life as simple as you are.

Chapter 2

Friendship

We learn to live with them and adapt to grow around them. Everybody needs at least one best friend to grow old with, one good friend to share daily news with, then a friend to watch your light shine. Outside of your Leaders, your friendships help mold you into who you are and will become. There's no way to predict a friendship. You must continuously evaluate the probability of which levels out of the three discussed categories broken down in my first sentence. Time and life brings on the correct labeling for which the peer is qualified to fit the description.

Let's talk about my personal experience of friends and how a few messed up my life. Yes, I have been bitten by snakes too, while on the other hand I have very few friends I can honestly call "friend". My bestfriend Gin and Vicki are my family. Without these two ladies in my life, trust me I wouldn't have any friends at all. I would be trapped in my apartment locked away like a hermit. Being stabbed in the back so many times by a so -called friend, caused me to turn cold to strangers and early depression.

I'm going to share an event that happen to me, I wished I had listen to my mother about this big black dumb snake in the beginning. She and I had been friends since 9th grade until 2001, the year the slimy snake bit me. I had a so-called boyfriend (which I should have never been involved with in the first place), he was a Mr. Right now, kind of guy. I would tell the big black snake about everything about my fake relationship, all the way down to the sex details. I have heard all the old friendship guidelines and my mother raised me with all her pass knowledge of choosing a good friend. But I was young and pure in heart and believed everybody was a Christian. I found out quickly there was evil around my soul, when I caught my first charge at age of 21. When that snake had sex with my supposed to be boyfriend, I flipped out. The war between me and her lasted for years, until I learned my lesson, to let those negative emotions go and watch how King Jesus got revenge on them both. It was fun watching or hearing their life fall apart, as it is today, they are still under my feet.

I have another example of bad friendships. This one was worse than my first situation only because we were friends that found out we are cousins. Now we just socialize and speak in spells. We bonded for years before she bit me. This WOMAN stole from my son, had sex with my boyfriend (a different one then before) and had a child from an ex-boyfriend that she knew was mines, but at the time of our relationship, acted as if she didn't like him or want him to her house. Boy, if that isn't a snake, then what do you call her? I don' t know how I had the strength to forgive her and still be involved with her, I think it was the fact that I truly love her children and still care about them now. Whatever the case may be, she's under my feet two.

I've learned a lot about friends from other people's experiences. The two that hurt me the most was the death of my uncle and a childhood friend. They were both good people and loved me. I still don't understand why somebody would kill either one or plan the death of these two good men. It happens at different times but in each case, their friend was there and the last person to see them alive, called for help, and went to their funeral. Goes to show how evil somebody can be in the flash of an cyc.

Enough about those negative ex friends of mine. I have just as many positive friends that I care less about those few bad apples. Now let me share a little insight about my bestie, Gin. She is a blessing to my life, we've been friends since high school and now she's like a sister to me. I can tell her anything and everything, this lady has never betrayed me in any way. Now that we have children and raising them up around each other, our friendship bond has grown stronger than ever. We have been through a lot of hard battles together and live through them all to look back at and laugh or cry.

My god-sister Vicki, now that's my heart. We are so close and have a beautiful bond together. We even had our first birth around the same time. She had twins and I had my first child which is my son Kese. Her and her family took me in at the age of 15. They treated me like I was a part of their family and still do till this day. I love each one of them as they are my own family members. My teenage years with Vicki were exciting. Her mother, who is my Godmother, had her hands filled with us all. There was Vicki, three sisters and my little sister hanging together while I was the baby sitter, lol. We all did everything together, even had a praise team that I put together being a member on the youth board at St. Paul Baptist church in Archer Fl. Vicki and I shared a lot of life experiences together when we were young. There's some space in between us now, but we still love each other as we always have. That's forever my God sister, and I don't play about her nor her family, as I am about my bestie Gin.

As you can see, friends help you become who you are by being involved in your everyday life. Have you ever heard "birds of the same feather flock together"? or "you are what you surround yourself with", both are true and two life rules that should be set in stone.

Here are some helpful thoughts that should help you overcome this stage of life:

- Don't seek violence on other people. Other words don't plan to do anything to somebody that you don't want life to bring back on yourself or your unborn planned family.
- Grudges are meant to be brushed off. Share your world with the right people and divide yourself from the wrong.
- Humbleness is patience wait for King Jesus to fight your battle. Some stuff doesn't make you, nor break you.
- You become what you attract. Remove yourself from around odd environments. Don't become a product of the wrong society.
- Good friends will always have your back and push you forward.
- Look forward to hearing news from close friends about the enemy's actions.
- Sometimes if you are acting right you'll be blessed

to retaliate back.
- Spend time with positive people, that brings out more positive energy within yourself.
- Never tell your friend all your business or personal secrets.
- Friends shouldn't share significant other with each other, nor backtrack the other leftovers.

Chapter 3

Family over everything

Family can either make you or break you. Or you can make them into the persons you need them to be for the rest of your life. Family can never be replaced no matter how hard you try. The Heavenly Father gave them to you for a reason. Don't think you have the most perfect family member in the world, you would be kidding yourself. It's the love, respect, trust, and caring bond shared between people that makes up family. When you don't have anybody in this world to run to or call on you should have family to back up and fight for you, no matter what.

Nobody's family is better than the next ones. The key to a strong family is acceptance, obedience, patients, strength, honor, truth, and worthiness to be yourself. What makes some families different is their source of higher power. Some worship the Heavenly Father and his son King Jesus, while some worship Satan/Devil, and there are some that don't believe in higher power, they just live in their moment on Earth. Whatever the case maybe, just love each other, that's all that matters to me.

From what I have learned, judging off my experience based on what I have learned about my family circle. We all worship the heavenly father and fear King Jesus. We all have our own personality which makes us compatible a lot but at the same time confrontational all the other times. At the end of the day, we all find command grounds to either agree or disagree. Finding common grounds to get along with each other, no matter what challenges that comes our way. We need and want each other's involvement in each other's lives, the key source of love is what keeps all of us growing up and helping one another through life.

Here are some helpful thoughts that should help you overcome this stage of life:

- Don't think for a second you'll never have to say sorry to nobody. If you get disrespected, ignore it and find a way to fix that issue.
- Never tell your family secrets to anybody. Some secrets are not to be shared with nobody for no reason. People can use it against you.
- Never expect somebody to listen to rules you don't want to follow by yourself.

- Get close to drama-free household members.
- Spend the holidays with your family, celebrate each other's birthdays and anniversaries and other life milestones together.
- Protect your family and pray for them rather than getting along or not.
- Show each other appreciation. One day we're here the next day we are gone.
- Value every gift given or received amongst each other. You never know how much it will be worth years later.

Chapter 4

Relationships

Never share your body with a person you'll regret in life later down the line. Every time you see them, you'll regret the stupid decision you had made back then. Pay careful attention to what you're dealing with and think about how far you can really see yourself going with them.

I would say it's better to marry before you lay up. What's the rush? Sex is a deadly sin in so many ways. I don't care what type of sex partner you chose, the problems and emotions that sex brings into a relationship are all still the same. For the moment, they seem like the right person. You want to marry each other. Let's make a family. Let's create our own world. Let's take over the world. All foolish ideals we think while together, a none holy relationship as Boyfriend and Girlfriend sexual partnership.

Why can't we be patience and wait for that perfect moment of unity as one whole to encounter having sexual love making desires to one another? What is the sole purpose of life? To create another life and bring them into our future. We have enough challenges living amongst each other, as it already is. We don't truly understand the full meaning of marriage, with all the research and living witness of unsuccessful marriages. There's got to be a sense of hoping there's some commend grounds (equal mind-frames, between two people, that believe in the same patterns of life principles as the other one does). Don't get me wrong sex is good. What you going to do once you're tired of having sex with that person and you realize your done breathing in the same hot air of each other? Cheat!, I guess.

Why once it's over you become evil and each other's haters? Why do we destroy somebody else only to realize later down the line that you'll find yourself needing that person's hand again in help? Then the games we play just to justify those washed up hidden emotions: angry, hurt, regret, disbelief, dead, and bitter. That mess doesn't solve nothing but good ole fashion headache and a bad name for yourself.

Here are some helpful thoughts that should help you overcome this stage of life:

- Don't wander off into distant land.
- Fears of love are not to be faced alone.

- Life has a lot of unthinkable blind curve balls waiting to come into play. No sex, less obstacles we'll have to live through.
- If you can avoid a bad relationship, do so by any means. If you can predict future problems, judging off, of what you're going through at that present moment, get out before it shows up at your front door.
- Some debts can't be erased. Just forgive and move on. "Troubles don't last always."
- If you don't get out in life and learn to live again, of course you're going to be heartbroken for the rest of your life.
- Just because you don't like something doesn't mean somebody else can't want them for themselves.
- Life is an endless journey of battles. Some bridges are meant to be broken. Burn them down and shut them out of your life. It's called the 'Deleting of lost love abuse'.
- Those bank account issues should be simple. Reward the sole survivor with their money and whatever else they wish for.

Chapter 5

Life Principles and Morals for a Female

Life is already challenging enough. This society stereotypes and is full of hidden racisms. Being a female plus a minority, some days can feel like a living nightmare or pure hell at some moments in time. It seems like we are born into a world of sin with dead weight on our backs. We grow into a woman but learn our true identities, within our middle age years of life, only if we make it that far in age living. Some of us learn our identities once we enter motherhood or early age marriages. Whatever the case maybe we all are different with some common grounds that allows us to get along in a social gathering, no matter what the vibe may be in the atmosphere.

Each one of the Heavenly Fathers creations including King Jesus has an intuition. For those that don't have a clue what an intuition is, it's the ability to understand something immediately, without the need for conscious reasoning. You just do it without thinking twice, other words. When a mother raises her child/children she builds a copy of herself based on her motherly intuitions and her vision on the child's future. All the facts about life are supposed to create your personality. The unique part about this process is we all have our own self-consciousness which makes you feel whole and supposed to make us independent/dominant beings. Some of us fall short of this self-righteous opportunity and become dependent on others to survive life. Which kind of woman are you a Leader or a Follower?

As a female, you set the tone for a lot of situations bad or good, we create the atmosphere in daily surroundings. Just think about if you think I'm wrong, the last time you were involved in anything, how many females were there and dealing with the situation. The world needs the female equation in order to exist, read the bible. We create our own world and pick who we are going to share it with throughout living our days and accouterment amongst others in our presences. That's what we call a circle.

Elderly woman is who they planned to be. Being an elder is the greatest gift from the Heavenly Father, you are a chosen one if you are over 60 and reading my book.

Here are some helpful thoughts that should help you overcome this stage of life:

- As a female, prepare yourself for the worst cases ever. We are built to gain the power of something.
- Ladies, know your worth. Believing in yourself will gain the correct attention of others.
- Mothers, love your children like nobody has ever loved you, they didn't ask for you and daddy to lay up and create them.
- Never allow others to direct your vision on how you plan on spending the rest of your life, or who you are going to spend it with. I bet they don't listen to your advice.
- Save money for yourself. Don't depend on others for nothing but love.
- Keep an open mind for growth. Watch your back for haters. Talk up on the things you're wishing for out of life.
- Never give a man your all.
- Don't allow one man the power to tear down your dream or control your future. If he is running a game on you, run it back on him. Eventually you'll

  win and he'll give in to your love.

Chapter 6

<u>It's not a Man's World</u>

Men are like a ball of clay. It takes a woman to mold them into life. Without the love of a good strong woman to teach them what life is all about, they would become a heartless being. Men's purpose in this world is to build, create life, provide for his family, and enjoy life with the homeboys. This is only speaking to the average male. Some do step outside their comfort zone and walk on the woman's side of life, trying to figure out their true personality. For the most part the ways of a man are all crazy and lost with love of a woman's touch.

You can't live with them nor without them. This is a true statement. The key to it is finding one half decent enough to transform into that ideal husband you dreamed of since a little girl. If you think you got him, let me help enlighten you on how to keep him closer later in this chapter.

Raising a man is hard during this time in life. You really need to step up and show your children some support. They will walk around in this world with the biggest hole in their heart for life if the father is not present and active. Why put that extra weight on your child? If you are a real man then prove it, by manning up to your responsibilities. Don't go shopping for your girlfriend's children when you got your baby momma in the shelter, struggling. You got on Jordan's and you children walking Walmart specials. If you are taking care of your children, then you are the man of the year. He's a keeper lady. That's your future baby daddy.

For the good men, that's following the rules to life and serving the Heavenly Father, I tip my hats off to you. Stay on track, and reach out to help others in your community become positive outlets as yourself. Rebuild your community and donate to your local charity organizations. You are so rich, then bless somebody back, and watch how life brings you more power and recognition. Be in the light and show out while doing it.

www.ingramcontent.com/pod-product-compliance
Lightning Source LLC
Chambersburg PA
CBHW070958120626
46546CB00004B/1674